Airplanes

A Journey Through the Sky

Jordan Birkholz

ISBN 979-8-9996742-0-3
Library of Congress Control Number: 2025917664

Published by Waypoint Publishing LLC
Colorado Springs, Colorado

Printed in the United States of America

For Alex and Luke,
May your dreams take flight
and your worries be light.

Have you ever wondered
Where airplanes go when they fly?
Do they zoom to far-off places,
Or just buzz around the sky?

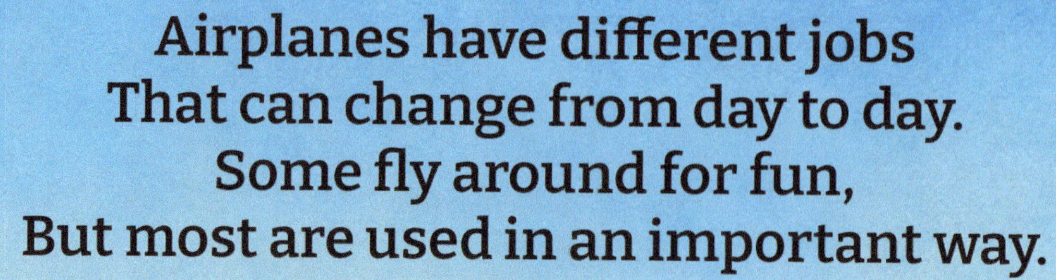

Airplanes have different jobs
That can change from day to day.
Some fly around for fun,
But most are used in an important way.

Airliners can transport hundreds
Of people from coast to coast.
Some go on vacation,
Some go to see the ones they love the most.

Cargo planes bring boxes,
Big and small, it's true.
Inside could be a teddy bear,
Or brand-new shoes for you.

Crop dusters are airplanes
That fly really low.
They spray farm fields
To help the plants grow.

Oil and gas are transported
Through pipelines on the ground.
Pipeline patrol is used
To make sure no leaks are found.

When a forest fire burns
And the ground is too hot,
A firefighting airplane
Drops water on the spot.

Skydive planes fly daredevils
That jump into the sky.
But before they start,
They need to go up really, really high.

AIR AMBULANCE

When someone gets hurt
And needs a hospital in a hurry,
An air ambulance is used
To get them there without worry.

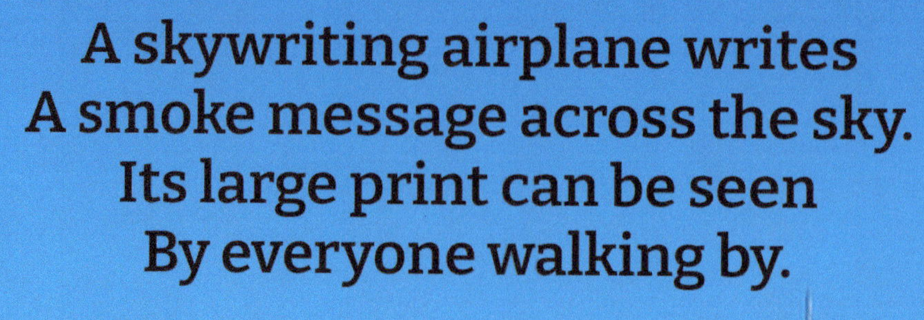

A skywriting airplane writes
A smoke message across the sky.
Its large print can be seen
By everyone walking by.

HI MOM

Now you know airplanes
Can do many different things.
But there's more to an airplane
Than the engine and the wings.

Airplanes need a pilot,
A job of the mighty few.

Some day you could be that pilot,
And see the world from a different view.

Airbus A330

McDonnell Douglas MD-11

Boeing B737

Canadair CL-415

Short 330

Beechcraft King Air 350

Air Tractor AT-802

P-51 Mustang

Cessna 172 Skyhawk

Boeing Stearman

Piper Super Cub